COVERED

COVERED

CAROLYN COLE

XULON PRESS

Xulon Press
2301 Lucien Way #415
Maitland, FL 32751
407.339.4217
www.xulonpress.com

Paperback ISBN-13: 978-1-66286-883-2

Table Of Contents

Acknowledgement

Thank you Father and bless your Holy name....To God be the Glory

Once again, I have been blessed with words of encouragement and love. I hope you will enjoy the poems contained in this book, as they are words given to me from a very reliable source, (Our Father)

As always, I would like to thank Pastor Bernard Curry and Elect Lady Linda Curry for being trustworthy influences in the lives at Mt. Zion United Church of God. And I say thanks for all the many prayers that they personally sent up to Heaven on my behalf during the time of my illness. I could not have been placed under a better leadership.

*Next, I would like to acknowledge the work of two very special ladies....
Elder Sandra Swinton and Elder Carolyn Chaney for the love they share every Wednesday afternoon hosting our prayer line. They are truly a blessing to many.*

Finally...my church family....they are the most loving and supportive group of people one could ever ask to know. It is a great joy and blessing to worship with them on Sunday mornings.

Hosea 10: 12

Sow for yourselves righteousness, reap the fruit of unfailing love, and break up your unplowed ground, for it is time to seek the Lord, until he comes and showers righteousness on you.

Hosea 14: 9

Who is wise? He will realize these things.
Who is discerning? He will understand them.
The ways of the Lord are right; the righteous walk in them, but the rebellious stumble in them.

The Letter

D ear Lord, our father of faith, have mercy on our backslidden land. For we are sinking deeper and faster, into the depth of forever darkness. Let us seek out the old paths of righteousness and truth. (The one our forefathers once walked.) Let us be reminded of how we once would kneel beside our bedside, calling upon your Holy name, and praying for the Holy Spirit to rest upon our souls. Lord, teach us how to face the demons that try to invade our thoughts, when all hope seems to subside. And when we ask for forgiveness, let our plea be heard by your precious and understanding heart. Father, we ask that you lend your ear to our request for peace and joy, as we raise our hands to you in praise. When the storms come, and we just can't see our way, let us be mindful, that we need but to call on your most precious and Holy name, and there you'll stand right in the mist, thus causing it to fade away. In this, we will remember your promise, that you'll never leave or forsake us and be ever so careful as to hold onto your most powerful hand. Oh Lord, please let us not forget to pray for the burden others carry, for in due season we all will be burden free. When the mountain seems too high and the valley seem so low, we ask that you speak peace over it. Father, let your angel of mercy fill our hearts with love and compassion for others, so that we may walk upright in your sight. For we know that we are indebted to you, and can never repay that debt, yet we strive to be obedient to you, your word and your will, so that one day, you will look upon us and know that your sons' death was not in vain. Let us remember how He walked up that hill to Calvary, hung on the cross in agony and pain for our sakes. And let us not *forget that you are the rock and cornerstone of our salvation. For these things we pray and say thank you. In the mighty name of Jesus. AMEN*

Sincerely, Your Children

What Would You Drop

Once in a while....Rare things happen......And you just can't figure them out
Such as sitting in church on a Sunday morn....And a stranger walk down the aisle
Now you know this is..........A Holy man..........By the aura that circles about
For you can see............The angel wings............ Flutter each time He stops.

Next you feel.......The atmosphere change......As He glides down to the front
Glances are given everywhere.........To see if you've seen what you thought
Then slowly He turns......And ask the question.....That somehow evaded your heart
"WHAT ARE YOU WILLING.....TO GIVE UP.....WHAT ARE YOU WILLING TO DROP ?

Are you willing to drop........ That attitude.......And all your wicked ways
In exchange for.............The kind of joy...........That only God can bring
And what about the jealousy..............envy................sins and shame
Tell me please......What will you drop.......What will you give up for Him ?

All through life.............You will learn.............Bad habits come every day
They come so easy.........To some of us...........And they always want to stay
But when we start........To walk with Christ......And the path that He has set
The anointing there...Will make them flee...For His blood has paid the debt

You need to learn.....To watch and wait....For you know not when He'll call

3

Covered

And rid yourself.........Of unrighteous things.............Rid yourself of them all
Disobedience.....greed.....pride and conceit..........Are all unsaintly you see
SO I ASK YOU AGAIN.....WHAT WILL YOU DROP......IN OUR
PRECIOUS SAVIORS NAME ?

Let Me Be Counted

Step by step by step.................Keep walking with the Lord
Prayer by prayer by prayer..................Keep talking with the Lord
Song by song by song....................Keep singing for the Lord
Day by day by day....................Keep serving the Lord

And whatever you so do............Keep praising His Holy name
The journey is easy......With the Lord......For He will never change

He's Able (One In The Same)

Because you had a very bad day.........Please don't take it to heart
For you have a better day ahead.........If you'll just let God be God
He healed the men of leprosy.......And the woman with the issue of blood
He saved the life of His servant Noah....On the day of the worlds' first flood

He paved the way for the Israelites....To escape from the enemies' hands
He parted the sea of water so deep....That opened on His command
He met the woman at the well.....And handled the situation there
He turned water into wine ....At one of the first gatherings held

He walked through fire with the Hebrew boys.........Delivered Daniel from
the lions' den
He kept some stones away from Paul....He held Jonah in the belly of the whale
He walked on water in the midst of a storm....Coming to the disciples rescue
HE'S ONE IN THREE.....WHEN ALL IS ONE.....THE SAVIOR FOR
ME AND YOU

For there's no limit to what God can do......If you'll just trust and believe
For He has done miraculous things...........For all who has love for him

Battle Cry

The Lord will fight....Your battles for you....If you'll only give Him a chance
By letting Him do......What He does best....That's being God himself
He'll form a silent quest inside.......That leads to a formation of hope
As it seals the void of certain defeat....When you feel your battles approach

He can hear the beat....As your heart doth cry....And can see the tears that fall
But His compassion......Is much stronger......Than all the battles that come
He'll blow out the candle of despair..........As it tries to light its way
Into your heart...........That's filled with pain.............. On any given day

For He is the Father of wisdom.........With the knowledge to carry through
If you will just.........REMAIN SILENT...........As He fights your battles for you

Him

*Oh, my Holy Spirit....Rest thineself upon Him....Him that makes you whole
Him that loves you forever....Bless his Holy name
Him who speaks to you....Consoles you....And makes you forever alive
Humble yourself before his presence...Acknowledge his everlasting power*

*Him who rescues me....When my body has no strength to fight...
Him who delights himself in my peace and my joy....And ask only for my
obedience....GLORY....GLORY....GLORY
Him who sits beside my bedside at night....And dares the darkness to enter
Even as I sleep.....He allows the light yet........To still shine in me.........
Thank you, My Precious Father,*

*Him who lays his ear upon my heart...........And listens to every cry of sorrow
And wipes every tear...Sending comfort to my soul....Praise his HOLY name
Never seizing to send new mercies and his most precious grace....on my every
awakening day
Him who has stamped his Holy name on my salvation....So that eternity will
be mine...Where there'll be no more mountains to climb...Or storms to rise*

*Him that loves me so much....That He sent his only son....TO DIE
HALLELUJAH........HALLELUJAH*

Just Like

Whenever you're in doubt.....About things you know you should do
I've already presented you with the plans.... In the book I sent to you
If you'll take the time to read it............And do just what it says
I promise you the solution..........To the questions in your head

For I've given to you some stories.......That should be easy to understand
Telling you about some people......... With the same problems you have.
I've written to you in parables...... Like the story of the prodigal son
And how he had lost everything............ But found his way back home

Or like the three Hebrew Boys....... And their amazing strength of faith
Not doing as the King had ordered........... For them there was no debate
You put too much thought into earthly things........And too much faith in man-
kind When all you need...Is to remember...That if you'll seek me...You will find

The Cross

His body was severely beaten........ Tired and burdened down
And through his unseen heart...........Was hope that lingered now
The cross held some things...............The naked eye could not see
It held his body captive..................Among other things

It held on to his being................Trying to imprison it there
It held his freedom of thought...........As the thorns stuck in his head
It held onto his breath ....As each gasp for air arrived
It held his seeing shut ....As the blood did fill his eyes

Imagine no salvation................ Being here to offer you
Imagine no freedom of choice........ But you know what you must choose
Imagine being crucified............ For something you did not do
Imagine having the whole world.......... Look differently at you

There are so many precious things............That the cross did hold
So I thank you Father...For making Him Holy....

And thank you for making Him strong

If I Could Hide

If I could hide my soul.........In any place I please
I'd hide it deep in Jesus.........Where my salvation is
I'd tuck it away in His glory.........Where peace and love abide
And let it rest forever.........In His presence it would hide

There it could see....A glimpse of the field....... Where the lilies of the valley grow
Where beauty and all of her splendor......... Are planted to make us strong
I could lay it in the angels' shadow.......So it could peek as He walked by
Wearing his robe and crown of glory.........That brightens the Heavenly sky

Or perhaps in the hem of his garment.......Where no outside force can touch
For there's safety there as promised........Where no storm dare not search
And yet there's always His wisdom.......For there I know I'd learn
The Holy ways of Jesus.........To help me overcome

If I could hide my soul.........In any place I please
I'd hide it deep in Jesus.......... Where my salvation is

Timely Prepared (To Be Read Slowly)

Nothing should be allowed there.........Nothing that can distract you from your thoughts
Close your eyes......Open your mouth......And let the words of thanks began
For the words are heartfelt and true......As you speak.......The love of Jesus is

FLOWING WARM IN YOUR VIENS
OH THE BLOOD OF JESUS...........IT WILL NEVER LOSE ITS POWER
The tears you shed......Are as soft sprinkles of hope....Let your voice be that of humbleness

TAKE YOUR TIME
The angels are there to speak the things......That you cannot utter
Your spirit fills with overwhelming joy.........It's as if.......It will spill over
You know He's there......You can feel his presence......It's so quiet and still
There is an undeniable peace........Surrounding you in this place

AND YOU KNOW YOU'RE BEING.................TIMELY PREPARED

Umm Umm Umm

If we could just peep.....Through the gate....And see the rewards of Heaven
We'd see all things.......Through the eyes.......Of Gods most precious angels
Oh what a sight.....We would behold......And much more than we expected
As we would look...........Upon His face...........And see His glory perfected

With righteousness held.....In his right hand.......And judgement in his left
We'll see our Savior sitting tall........With salvation around his neck
Angels all bowed......In snowy white...........With Holiness on each side
Holding hands.....With purity in hearts......As their wings spread open wide

As Grace is holding.....Her staff of favor....And Mercy his rod of forgiveness
We'll see three rings of glory shine...........Significant of the Trinity
And yes we'll see the beautiful home.........Not made by human hands
But instead it's held.....Together by faith.........Where love was used as nails

If we could peep........Through the gate.......And see the rewards of Heaven
We'd be compelled..........To live better.........And pay more close attention
For we would want......To change our ways......As He has prepared a home
For us to live.................In His presence.................Singing

UMM UMM UMM UMM UMM

13

Judge Ye Not

Have you ever talked to God.....And asked, "Why is this happening to me"?
Before you take it upon yourself.......Trying to answer that question
Have a talk with wisdom first.............Before you make assumptions
Listen to what she has to say..............About things you do not know
As you will find....In your darkened mind....That life's not easy for God

Try sitting in........His place for a day....Receiving all kinds of requests
And see if you........Could do His job............Without anger or regret
None is worthy.........For this is true........And it's really hard to accept
So, he's being accused............Of not caring..........Because you're upset

For He must listen to all our calls............As He's a different one to many
Yet He's all in one...........And one in all............For He is the Holy Trinity
For He's not one.......And he's not two........Yes, He is the mighty three
As they all have power...In their hands........And love for all.......You see

For you're not the only one with trials...........Some more so than you
So, give Him time........And stay in prayer........And just trust in what he do
And whatever it is........You need from Him..........Stop judging and receive
Cause the answer to......Your earlier question......Is answered if you believe

BECAUSE WHEN IT'S ALL SAID AND DONE........ 'YOU'RE JUDGING HIM"

Out Of Time

On that day of reckoning..........There'll be nowhere to hide
Run sinners run........ ....You'll hear that trumpet sound
No mountain........No rock.......No stone..........Will be left here unturned
On that day of reckoning......... You'd better run sinners run

I can see His chariots coming........On clouds upon darkened sky
Angels racing beside Him.............Crying out the mercy cry
Wings all linked together...........As to make sure the chain is kept
And a long train of sorrow..........Upon the riders' belts

The swift feet of the horses burning........Their hoofs are a blaze of fire
And the chariots keep on rolling..........While their riders never tire
Run sinners run................For no hiding place can be found
You'll hear the noise of a mighty wind......As that last trumpet sounds

BUT IT'S TOO LATE FOR YOU TO RUN...FOR TIME HAS RUN
OUT OF TIME !

Saving Shadow

There is a storm arising............So inside you must go
To hide yourself in Jesus..............Where no storm can come
When the enemy comes to haunt you........Leaving things you cannot fix
Remember you have a savior...........That knows the enemy's tricks

Go inside your closet............Where your savior you will meet
For there He has a covering............That the enemy cannot see
There is a shadow that lingers..........Within your secret place
Belonging to the heart of Jesus..............Holding you as you pray

For there you can tell Him your problems.........And He will hear your cry
As the rolling thunder clashes............And your troubled clouds pass by
Go inside that room of Glory..........Where His spirit rest
And on your knees.....Call out His name.........And that shadow of peace will hear

Lord wrap your arms around me..........For I have a need to feel your peace
As I pray to you my Father..........In this room so filled with Grace
Lord help my feet to flee..........From the enemy encamping me
Show me how to run and hide..........Hide myself in thee.

He that dwelleth in the secret place of the most high....
Shall abide under the shadow of the almighty

He Is

DO YOU KNOW HE WALKED ON WATER !!!!

Wherefore God also highly exalted him, and given him a name above
EVERY NAME

For you must believe and acknowledge Him ...For the greatness He possess
And recognize.........His position..........As the king in which He is.

So many people are crying now......Asking...."What must I do to be saved"?
And tho that question's been asked before....The answer is still the same
You must be born once again.........And give up the worldly things
You must learn to sacrifice ....Some things you think you need

When all these things in reality............ Is just a simple ploy
To blind you and deceive you.................Making an unholy noise
For all the things you thought you knew...Is now a shadow of light...So dim
And no longer can they...Block your blessings...Nor wonders yet to be seen

You see....He is......The way to be saved......He and HE alone
For his Holy word is so full of truth.......As He guides your footsteps on.

Glory Shine

Teach me to be more trusting..........In your decisions Lord
Let your light shine on me..............As it saturates my soul
For you are my rock and refuge....The calm in the midst of my storm
Peace in my heart of sorrow........Strength when I'm not strong

For my flesh and heart might fail me....But in you I can trust...I know
As there's no darkness in you............But a heavenly light aglow
Yet as a fly.........Is on whitewashed wall.......And I....A spec in your sight
Casting a shadow oh so small.............Please shine your Glory Light

And as the blood that flows...Through angels' veins..... Was a ransom to set us free
So is our hope...When entangled with grace...Will make your blessings appear
For we know that you........Will provide.......What we cannot purchase now
Which is indeed...............Eternity...............And your everlasting joy divine

Only Your Amazing Grace

Why Do You Think I Came ?

Why do you think I came?............To watch you waste your lives?
Why do you think I came?...............To let sin abide?

I came that you may live..........In a place of peace and joy
Not for you to perish..............In an unholy and sinful world

I came so you could see things.........Through the heart and eyes of God
I came so you would not be blind........To the work of the unsaved one

I came to tell you of a place.........Where there's days upon days of hope
And to tell you of your Father..........Who has so much more to show

When our Father looked down...And saw this place...It hurt His eyes to see
All the terrible things going on..........So He decided to send me

So I came to give you a better view.........Of things yet left to come
In the place that we call Heaven..........Our new and eternal home

And last....He wants me to tell you.......To stand tall and please be still
So I came to tell you He loves you.........And know that his love is real

Awaken Me

Awaken me from my slumber Lord...Early in the morn
Let your angel of mercy touch me....As you so gently call
Awaken my mind......To recognize you.........In every move I make
For I want to be stirred......By your Holy Spirit...In every step I take

Let my joy in you......Continually bloom.....So that outwardly it will show
That the depth of your compassion................Inwardly continues to grow

And as the day goes on.................... Let me not forget
To be forever thankful ....For each and every breath

Please guide my footsteps one by one......To prevent my fall or stumble
Making sure the path is kept...............That's set right there before me
Hold my hand...........So that I won't wander.........Into a trap of deceit
That yet was set for another...............Into a way not meant for me

When I think of how much you love me............It's such a precious peace
To know that you're always present...........And my soul can rest with ease

See As You Do

People won't always see the same....Or think the same as you
Thus causing you.....To doubt sometimes......And try to see as they do
But theirs is not the way to go.....Or bend your thoughts to change
For your way was given.....To you....To honor....As well as for you to claim

When a vision is placed....Within your heart....It's put there for a reason
It's meant for you to carry out......For the fulfillment of the season
You cannot please everyone.......And there's only one you should consider
And that's our savior.......Jesus Christ........The one who can deliver

For He is the one for you to please....And He is the one that listens
To all your problems and things you fear.....Yes.... He is the only decision

You cannot change....What's given to you .....From the one who sits on high
For He is the one.....That watches over us..........As time is flashing by
So don't delay......Or look to others.....For from them it has been concealed
Instead it's your........Gifted blessing..........That God wants you to reveal

We Cry Sometimes

It's such a divine passion of peace......To release the tears we shed
All filled with the Holy spirit of Jesus......And the anointing that He has

Mighty are the tears......And strong is the strength....
From every tear that falls....From the eyes of the Holy Saint

Mighty are the tears that fall....For they hold what we can't speak
And silently they can wash away......All the pain in which we feel

For they will always be remembered.....In the mind of the Holy Lamb
With grace and peace abounding.....From the sacred and great "I AM"

Mighty are the tears we shed....For they can clear the heart of pain
And bring new joy to our very soul.....From that thing that lingered there

Our Way Back

Claiming front row...........First seat only............Some will sit so pretty
With the impression.......Of being rich.......Yet they cannot take it with em
So, whether you're rich.......Or whether you're poor.......We'll all be judged together
For we all must travel......The same old road......To get back....To our creator

For we as Christians.......Must learn to live.......Our lives all joined together
Before we reach the Pearlie Gates.........To live as one in Heaven
We cannot carry........The hatred in.......Or an unbelieving heart of stone
As the gates will close......And you're turned around.....To walk in darkness alone

You cannot judge.......Your sisters or brothers......For you do not have that pleasure
For what you use.......As a scale for others.......By that......You too will be measured
As we all are working..........Our way back ....With burdens upon our shoulders
*Lets put aside......All petty antics......Join hands.......And praise **HIM** forever*

The Crossroad

Sometimes you.......Can find yourself..........At a crossroad in your life
Trying to remove.......All distractions.......In hope that He'll meet you there
Then you'll pray for strength to believe......And the conviction to obey
Looking back over the mountainside.......That He has brought your way

There you'll learn to seek his face.........Amid your darkened storms
Your heart and soul will open wide......As your quest for truth doth come
You'll think of the valleys and the hills......That He has brought you through
And how you made it over...............As He was there with you

For at the crossroad you will find...He is the branch...And you are the vine

For at that point, you'll feel Him............Clear confusion in your soul
And you'll learn to pray in the spirit..........As He returns you to the mold
Yes....He'll change your way of thinking....In this place where your troubles unfold
And you'll be glad He met you.............Down at the old crossroad

Misunderstood

It's not being afraid of the unknown......But knowing is what terrifies them......
It's not that they take what you say the wrong way....It's that they know what you
say is true.......So, they try to silence you somehow.........Because they know that
enormous value of wisdom that you carry...... May someday just seep through.

You're a praying soul...To whom God replies....And such an admirable trait to
have....Carrying burdens that do not belong to you......But on that day.......

GLORY...GLORY....GLORY*....When you cross over......They'll look and see*
that you're gone....And with sorrow filled hearts....They'll wished they had
listened......

To the one they misunderstood.

The Vision

The prayer room is the place to be....For things to happen miraculously
Where hearts and minds all fit together...As many blessings are expected

Oh, wretched eyes of mine did see....A vision of His Majesty
There He stood.......As still as could be.....From behind him he reaches

Within His hand there is a string............As strong as a rope can be
He pulled it over his head with ease.....Around and about it covers me

And all that is....In the room....Is covered by the bowl of blood
In which he turns....With a rapid stir.... Under a blinding......light above

Oh, wretched eyes of mine did see
A vision of His Majesty
All dressed in snowy white ......You see
All still....As still.....As still.......As Can be

Listen

When the Holy Spirit speaks to you......It's no longer you doing the thinking
Welcome Him..........Open heartedly..........For now He's doing the speaking
He'll tell you of some things..............That are ready to unfold
He'll teach you how to open up.............And pray what's in your soul

Let your mind be quiet..........Then you'll clearly hear His voice
In the stillness of His silence.........So warm.......So loving.........So calm
He'll tell you of a place...........Where pain does not exist
And all about the glory.........That embrace our Fathers' face

He'll tell you of a land.............Where the pastures are oh so green
And the valleys have streams of water.......With a soft and gentle smell
He'll talk about our shepherd............This wonderful Holy man
That's waiting with open arms............For He is the rock that stands

For there you'll find our savior.............With all that He has promised
Where our loved ones await us there........In this land of milk and honey
And there you'll find.........All peace of mind.........And a Holy love inside
Where all the warmth........Of the Holy Trinity.........So patiently resides

Lion With A Cloven Tongue

Lord, please let me be......Inclined to hear.......The words in which you speak
Let the cloven tongue......Of your Holy Spirit......Rest itself upon me
For your power is like....A roaring lion....So mighty....So strong....So bold
So let the cloven tongue......Of your Holy Spirit......Rest upon my soul

For I want to be filled ....With that burning fire....That's sent to set me free
That reminds me of your sweet...sweet spirit....That always so quietly speak
And let me be able....To lift mine eyes....To the hill where my help is kept
And taste the water....From the river Jordan....Where I know your healing
has touched

Let every footstep that I take.........Fit the footprints you have made
For the future that you have for me......To live a Holy life always

For you say we are.....To pray in the spirit......So this prayer I offer to you
For you are.......That roaring lion........That possess that cloven

Tongue of truth

Let The Service I Give.....Speak For Me

My Heavenly Father..................Please hear my plea.....
Let the service I give ....Speak for me
May the words I write..................Touch someones' heart
And produce a soul.....................With a Holy Ghost spark

And let that spark......Start a fire......Of spiritual awakening unknown
In a blending of love......With a heartfelt shove......That's so blinding strong
Let the service I give.....................Speak for me
Oh Lord my father.........................Hear my plea

And let that heartfelt shove......So blinding strong......Lead them to victory
As the road they take......With every step..........Have them come closer to thee
Let the words I write.........Touch someones' heart.............As they read the words
from thee.....
Let them touch their souls.....Like a fiery dart......Filled with blessings unseen

Bring forth your words............. My Father I plea....

LET THE SERVICE I GIVE........SPEAK FOR ME

Too Little.....Too Late

Things we need to do today..............Should not be put off for tomorrow
For it's better to do it right away.........To decrease all pain and sorrow

Remember to say "I love you"
To someone you love today
Don't hold the words..... Deep down inside
As time just slips away

Don't wait to say "I meant to"
Thinking you have more time
Keeping the undone works with you
And many tasks undone

People you need to talk to
Hurry and don't delay
For that conversation........ Might be needed
To save a soul today

When an apology is warranted
Do it right away
Don't let it be said you waited
It may be "too little... too late"

When you awake each morning.....Before your feet can touch the floor
Thank your Father for keeping you....And giving you one day more.

Thank You

We were taught to say "Thank You"....As a sign Of love and respect!
*When we say "Thank you".....**He** responds......By showing us righteousness*

Lord grant me the understanding ....That I need in my daily walk
And thank you Father for loving me.........For your mercy I have sought
Please show me the way of your wisdom........So that I may follow
As my hope is now.......Resting in you.......For a new day called tomorrow.

Thank you, Father, for letting me see.......... The dusk of this day unfold
And thank you Lord... For your saving grace.....As my future you do hold
I thank you Father....... For the gift of speech.......So that I may pray to you
And glorify your Holy name..........And the miraculous things you do.

Thank you, Lord.........For healing me............And allowing me more time
For now, I know......To know you better......Is the most precious gift I own
*But most of all:..... I thank you Jesus..........**For your endurance on the cross***
*For your unselfish love ....For each soul that day....**Can never be forgotten***

Prayer Before Sharing

Say a prayer before you reveal.......Something that you hold sacred
If it's to be told....Then let it be shown...Through prayer and supplication

Some secrets are meant....... To be kept.........And some need to be shared
Holding them down deep inside........Can turn them from thoughts to tears
What we try to hide from others.............Can consume our hearts with fear
Sharing our thoughts....With someone else....Could release a binding there

Secrets kept within ones heart............Are like old garments in a closet
That we proclaim......... One day we'll wear......But put back on the hanger
For it must be brought........... Into the open.......For other people to hear
And it could be............. A testimony..............To help someone else to heal.

For some secrets can......... Boil and brew......Impacting chaos in our minds
Making no sense of right from wrong.............And can fester over time
So pray to God......And He'll let you know.......On what to be silent or speak
Or whether your secret is to be shared..............Or remain a secret kept

When You See Me

Don't look at me all funny.......Cause I don't praise like you
You don't know my story............Or what I've had to go through
When you see me shouting............Don't laugh at my Holy dance
It's my way of saying............ "Thank you"..... For another chance

When you see me crying..........It's not because I'm sad
It's just me being happy.........For the grace and mercy he has
And when you hear....A change in my voice......Or the way that I am speaking
It's the Holy Spirit filling my mouth..........With what He's really thinking

And as you see me walking..........Don't mind the steps I take
For I'm following the footsteps of Jesus.......And all the footprints He makes
For the blueprints are carefully made.......For the life He's planned for me
And I will try to stay in step............Although I don't always see

So when you see me smiling.........It's for the love I have within
Knowing that my precious Savior.........Is still holding me close in him

I Decided

I decided long ago.........That I would follow you
I knew then..........I had to say no.........To the things I used to do
I decided to turn and run.........From the places I used to go
The things I thought I knew back then........I found I didn't know
I decided to find some good ....Even in someone that's bad
Although I must admit sometimes.......It's a hard and tedious task

Yes....I decided long ago......That you were the choice for me
And that you would lead and guide me...If I would just trust and believe
I decided to look above.......To see what maybe I'd missed
And lo and behold.........Look at the blessings.......Given to me as gifts

I decided that I need to pray a little harder, sing a little stronger and laugh a little longer. I decided to make my good, better......and my better my best. I decided to make God my all and all, and in doing so, I decided to make a joyful noise in spite of all the things that make this world so sad.

I decided just to be happy............By just being me!!!!

Preparation

We did not know when we arrived......And will not know when we leave
All we know.......Is we're traveling through...... This time and earthly realm.

Our Father packed our bags for us
When at first........ We were born
He placed a lot of things in there
So we could find our way back home

He placed a sense of awareness......Into our soul so deep
To keep us alert, and well-rehearsed.......For the unknown troubles we'd meet

He placed a sense of loyalty......Into our very being
So obedient we would stay......... And on Him we'd always lean

He placed a sense of love.........Within our hearts with care
To get along with each other............While we're still living here

He gave us a book of directions....................To help us understand
That He had prepared us long ago................To return unto to Him again

Someone Else

Have you ever seen someone.................That really caught your eye
And secretly wished............It to be you...........Way deep down inside
You'll let your feelings go astray..........Becoming blind to what you see
Forgetting God makes no mistakes....And you're who He wanted you to be

We have a tendency.........To forget.......How carefully we were made
From the fleshly frame.....In which we're in......To the color of hair we have
When God decided to place you..........Within your mother's womb
He knew exactly what you needed..........To be the person you are

He spoke the words of wisdom and love.............Into your tiny heart
For He knew that it would grow one day......To bring light within your soul
He knew what color.......To paint your skin......And the smile to fit your face
He knew how much strength to add.........As He put everything else in place

He made you to be..........One of a kind.........And this will always be true
For you're the only one He made..........To be...........The one and only you
It's always best to be yourself..............No matter where you roam
As God has made you..... Holy and special.....Now who could ask for more.

Just One Look

All the answers.... To your healing needs.......For upon my back is written
And salvation was found in my blood....As each stripe on that day was given
Open your eyes.........Take a look..........And be amazed at what you see
*For on my back....They signed their names....Not knowing my back was **"HE"***

They did not know....Their names were sealed....... In my blood that day
They did not know....That I would remember........ Each ones' angry face
So, I took them to the cross with me....For they did not know their deed
For every stripe.......My back received ......Would help someone in need

Take a look and see.....How this paved the way......For you to overcome
Just one look....... Is all that's needed.........And then you'll understand
That on my back........The writers left........The prints of unknowing odds
That will be as a reminder.....To everyone.....That I am the son of God

For on that day...They did not know...That their bad would turn into good
Never knowing... Each stripe they gave......Was a remedy for someones soul

I THANK YOU JESUS FOR THE STRIPES YOU TOOK FOR ME

Let Me Lord

Empower me Lord......To possess.........A drop of oil from your wisdom seed
And be a servant........To you my father.........Wherever there is a need

Let me focus on the things.............Which you have prepared for me
To overcome unsaintliness...........Which I know......Is not pleasing to thee
Let me stand on solid ground.............Where the soil is rich with hope
Where I can hear.......All that's said........From the place of the Holy Throne

Let my heart..........Of burdens lie............Upon your shoulders strong
Because I know............My love for you...........Is for you and you alone
Let the Holy Spirit fill my soul...........As He rest in the chambers there
And keep me on top ....Of all the things.......That secretly awaits me here

Let your angel of Mercy.....Guide my steps.... As I so graciously walk
Let your angel of Grace....Extend her arms....To catch me when I fall

Let me not dwindle.........In anything........That concerns my faith at work
And let me rush..........To your every call...........That keeps my mind alert
For I know that if I'm allowed to do...................Most or all these things
I'll be better equipped.....And able to accept......Whatever this life may bring

Just Here

We are not......Of this place....We are just here
To spend our time........Praising our Lord

We are just here

We belong to a higher source.......We are just here
To let everyone, know......They have a choice.

We are just here.

So, while we're here........Lets live and let live
And always remember one thing
We are just here........... To get into practice

Of how we're supposed to live.

Water To Wine

There was a wedding at Cana ......Where Jesus and his disciples were guest
Everyone was laughing and drinking....And I imagine enjoying themselves
Then Mother Mary noticed a change....And decided to tell her son
"The wedding seems to be slowing down...Because all of the wine is gone".

He asked, "Why are you telling me this......For my time has not yet come"?
But by one mighty......Wave of his hand......His first miracle was performed.
He said .... Fill the empty jars with water...Up to the very brim
And into wine ....It did turn........Thus showing his power within.

The water had so quickly changed......Into something so smooth that day
For I could see him wave his hand...............Atop of the jars of clay
For the wine was made by Holy hands...........With truth and confidence
By the one and only Jesus Christ.............And his glorious omnipotence

For the taste of it....surely did please........ As they sat and sipped away
Saying this is the best.. Wine we've tasted... At this wedding here on today
And as they continued to sip and drink..........The disciples faith had grown
As they had witnessed the miracle ....And knew what had been done

For the things that happened on that day...........Was known only by a few
And Jesus himself had cleared the way......For he had more miracles to do
For He had changed the atmosphere ....From a wedding so blah to divine
When He had turned those jars of water...Into jars of mighty fine wine

Praise Be

Lord don't move the mountain............But give me the strength to climb
Don't remove the stumbling blocks............But grant me mercy to learn
For you are the Father of wisdom.........And the Savior of knowledge too
And we will give you......Our all and all......Cause all things belong to you

Praise be......................To the Lord.............To God our loving Savior
Who bears our burdens daily...........For you're the lamb of our redemption
Boost our faith....Within you Lord......During the tenderness of your silence
Causing us.......To hear your word........Even during your sovereign quiet

Lord teach us how.......To forever follow........And never by the wayside fall
Let us not................Step out of order..........Ears open to your every call
And we thank you for.......Your mighty voice......That breaks through every wind
That speak peace....To our souls......Saying **"PEACE YOU WILL BE STILL"**

For within you we all are conquerors.............As we build our house on you
And your foundation......Is strong and sturdy....Built on your love for truth
So don't dismiss us............From your heart...........Where all salvation lies
For you are the rock......Of Holiness.......That dwells down deep inside

Serving Notice

Our Father says...."Stop and Listen".......For there is something that I have found
The world is moving much too fast.........And I'll have to slow it down
For there are some......That will not listen......To the words in which I have spoken
There are some........With the Bible beside them........And never is it opened.

There are some....That go through the day....Without giving me a thought
There are some......That forget to pray.........As their lives add up to naught
And there are some....Whose eyes are shut...For they refuse to look and see
The troubled world in which they live.......And they close their ears to me.

For I promised you..........I'd never leave
But you need to change your ways,
And only to me................should you cleave
And remember me every day.

Restless Prayer

When sleep refuse you.......late at night........And rest is not to be found
Stretch out your arms in total praise..........And talk to God for awhile

Father teach me how....To decrease self....As each of your days grow old
And let your spirit increase Lord...........Set a fire deep down in my soul

Teach me how to humble myself..........And convict me of my repentance
Send a wind of change....To come my way.....Blowing away any sinfulness

Grant me an attitude of humility ....For I am your servant Lord
And as the angels of Heaven....Rise up and sing...Let your mercy on me fall

Fill me with your Holy Spirit..........So that I may walk in peace
Shine your light........To cover my soul...........As I grow in your holiness

Let the grass..............Under my feet.............forever remain green
And hold onto me..........My precious Savior.......For I am forever redeemed

Trying Times

Sometimes things.......Will come our way....That we can't understand
But we must remember...And not lose hope ....For He's the healer of our pain
When we release.......Our thoughts of trouble.......And we leave them there
He'll answer us.......As we call.........For He hears........Our cry in prayer

For trying times will come our way...........Filling our lives with confusion
But we can't rely......On our decisions......Coming to the wrong conclusion
Instead we can count........On our Father God........He was there from the beginning
And He foresaw the issue coming....And right there....He started it's ending

He knows each one of our trials..........And can call them name by name
So he is the answer........To each of them..........Because He never change
He knew what you would face..............In your life to come
That is the reason.........Jesus went to the cross........So you can trust in HIM

And now it's time to show your faith..........As tears stream from your eyes
For He has already...........Let you see..........He's right there by your side
And this is the time.....For worship and prayer.....Believing without a doubt
As He will hold you close to Him................Healing and working things out

Speak To Me

On one day they dressed my Jesus......... In a robe made up of hate
It was made from the threads of anger.......Prepared for our Saviors' sake
For the powerful blood from Jesus............ Turned that purple robe to red
As did the same with the thorns............That were placed upon His head

And if this robe could speak to me...... I can imagine what it would say
"For I am the one upon His back....... Embracing His blood today
And in my Savior the strength is felt......As the glory and splendor are too
And the thorns that are placed upon His head.... Heard His prayers go through

For they do not know about this man....... For whom they've done this to
For the blood He shed withholds a strength...... That cleanses the sins....Of both
me and you"

Precious Time

Look in the mirror........And you will see......How your appearance has changed
And think of where.....He brought you from......To where you're placed today
And thank Him for your bad times..........Which led you to your good
Say a prayer......In a soften whisper.......When you've done the best you could

Time........ Precious time...........Is one of His greatest gifts
As God took time to make us..............In the image of himself
Time.........Precious time............Should never be a waste
For sometimes it seems....................So little of it......
So, what you have........"EMBRACE"

Jesus took time to come here..................Spreading His fathers' words
He took the time to go to the cross................Shedding His precious blood
Time..............Precious time................Be diligent in how you pray
Do the servants' work of Christ..........And be thankful everyday

Posibilities

Rolling clouds of mercy
Young shoulders..........Old souls
Chariot wheels turning
Watching the north wind blow

The mighty rushing waters
That cover the mountains' ledge
Are miraculous things you will see
If you watch the Masters' hand

Slowly days will pass away
As the time keeps rolling on
And you'll not see......It coming at all
Yet another day is gone

Rolling clouds of mercy
Young shoulders..........Old souls
Chariot wheels turning
Watching the north wind blow

Read All About It

Read All About It....Part One

*1ˢᵗ **Samuel 2:6-10 & 16:7***

2:6....The Lord brings death and makes alive; he brings down to the grave and raises up.

2:7....The Lord sends poverty and wealth; he humbles and exalts.

2:8....He raises the poor from the dust and lifts the needy from the ash heap; he seats them with princes and has them inherit a throne of honor. "For the foundations of the earth are the LORD'S; upon them he has the world.

2:9....He will guard the feet of his saints, but the wicked will be silenced in darkness. "It is not by strength that one prevails.

2:10...those who oppose the Lord will be shattered. He will thunder against them from heaven. The Lord will judge the ends of the earth." He will give strength to his king and exalt the horn of his anointed."

16:7....But the Lord said to Samuel, "Do not consider his appearance or his height, for I have rejected him. The Lord does not look at the things man looks at. Man looks at the outward appearance, but the Lord looks at the heart."

Read All About It….Part Two

PSALM 18:1-3 & 18:27-30

18:1....*I love you, O Lord, my strength.*

18:2....*The Lord is my rock, my fortress and my deliverer; my God is my rock, in whom I take refuge. He is my shield and the horn of my salvation, my stronghold.*

18:3....*I call to the Lord who is worthy of praise, and I am saved from my enemies.*

18:27...*You save the humble but bring low those whose eyes are haughty.*

18:28...*You, O Lord, keep my lamp burning; my God turns my darkness into light.*

18:29...*With your help I can advance against a troop; with my God I can scale a wall.*

18:30...*As for God, his way is perfect; the word of the Lord is flawless. He is a shield for all who take refuge in him.*

Read All About It....Part Three

Isaiah 1:18-20 &2:22

1:18..."Come now, let us reason together," says the Lord. "Though your sins are like scarlet, they shall be as white as snow, though they are red as crimson, they shall be like wool.
1:19...If you are willing and obedient, you will eat the best from the land;
1:20...but if you resist and rebel, you will be devoured by the sword." For the mouth of the Lord has spoken.

2:22....Stop trusting in man, who has but a breath in his nostrils. Of what account Is he

Read All About It....Part Four

Jude 1:21-25

1:21....Keep yourselves in God's love as you wait for the mercy of our Lord Jesus Christ to bring you to eternal life.

1: 22....Be merciful to those who doubt

1: 23....snatch others from the fire and save them; to others show mercy, mixed with fear-hating even the clothing stained by corrupted flesh.

1:24....To him who is able to keep you from falling and to present you before his glorious presence without fault and with great joy....

1: 25....to the only God our Savior be glory, majesty, power and authority, through Jesus Christ our Lord, before all ages. Now and forevermore! Amen.

Read All About It….Part Five

Titus….3:12-15

3:12….See to it brothers, that none of you has a sinful, unbelieving heart that turns away from the living God.

3:13……But encourage one another daily, as long as it is called Today, so that none of you may be hardened by sins deceitfulness

3:14….we have come to share in Christ if we hold firmly till the end the confidence we had at first.

3:15….As has just been said: "Today, if you hear his voice, do not harden your hearts as you did in the rebellion"

Read All About It Six

GENESIS 1:27-31

1: 27.....So God created man in his own image, in the image of God he created him; male and female he created them.

1: 28....God blessed them and said to them, "Be fruitful and increase in number; fill the earth and subdue it. Rule over the fish of the sea and the birds of the air and over every living creature that moves on the ground."

1: 29.....Then God said, "I give you every seed-bearing plant on the face of the whole earth and every tree that has fruit with seed in it. They will be yours for food.

1:3o.....And to all the beasts of the earth and all the birds of the air and all the creatures that move on the ground- everything that has breath of life in it-I give every green plant for food." And it was so.

1:31.....God saw all that he had made, and it was very good. And there was evening, and there was morning—the sixth day.

Read All About It......Seven

1 John....1:5-7 and 3:1-2

1:5....This is the message we have heard from him and declare to you: God
Is light; in him there is no darkness at all.

1:6.....If we claim to have fellowship with him yet walk in the darkness, we
lie and do not live by the truth.

1:7.....But if we walk in the light, as he is in the light, we have fellowship
with one another, and the blood of Jesus, his Son, purifies us from all sin.

*3:1....How great is the love the Father has lavished on us, that we should be
called children of God! And that is what we are! The reason the world does
not know us*
Is that it did not know him.

*3:2....Dear friends, now we are children of God, and what we will be has not
yet been made known. But we know that when he appears, we shall be like him,
for we shall see him as he is.*

Read All About It Eight

Romans 14:11-13 & 14:19

14:11.....It is written "As surely as I live," says the Lord "every knee will bow before me; every tongue will confess to God."

14:12....So then, each of us will give an account of himself to God.

14:13.....Therefore let us stop passing judgement on one another. Instead, make up your mind not to put any stumbling block or obstacle in your brothers" way.

14:19.....Let us therefore make every effort to do what leads to peace and to mutual edification.

Read All About It Nine

1 PETER.....3-5 &....8-9 ....1 PETER....2:22-25

1:3.....Praise be to the God and Father of our Lord Jesus Christ! In his great mercy he has given us new birth into a living hope through the resurrection of Jesus Christ from the dead,

1:4.....and into an inheritance that can never perish, spoil or fade—kept in heaven for you,

1:5.....who through faith are shielded by God's power until the coming of salvation that is ready to be revealed in the last time.

2:22....."He committed no sin, and no deceit was found in his mouth."

2:23......When they hurled their insults at him, he did not retaliate; when he suffered, he made no threats. Instead he entrusted himself to him who judges justly.

Read All About It Ten

Proverbs....8: 1-2...5-8....10-11....34-36

8:1....Does not wisdom call out? Does not understanding raise her voice?
8:2....On the heights along the way, where the paths meet, she takes her stand;

8:5....You who are simple, gain prudence; you who are foolish, gain understanding.
8:6....Listen, for I have worthy things to say; I open my lips to speak what is right.
8:7....My mouth speaks what is true, for my lips detest wickedness.
8:8....All the words of my mouth are just; none of them is crooked or perverse.

8:10....Choose my instruction instead of silver, knowledge rather than choice gold.
8:11....for wisdom is more precious than rubies, and nothing you desire can compare with her.

8:34....Blessed is the man who listens to me, watching daily at my doors, waiting at my doorway.
8:35....For whoever finds me finds life and receives favor from the LORD.
8:36....But whoever fails to find me harms himself, all who hate me love death.

Read All About It…. Eleven

PHILIPIANS 4:4-8

4:4….Rejoice in the Lord always, I will say it again; Rejoice!

4:5….Let your gentleness be evident to all. The Lord is near.

4:6….Do not be anxious about anything, but in everything, by prayer and petition, with thanksgiving, present your request to God.

4:7….And the peace of God which transcends all understanding, will guard your hearts and minds in Christ Jesus.

4:8….Finally brothers, whatever is true, whatever is noble, whatever is right, whatever is pure, whatever is lovely, whatever is admirable—-if anything is excellent or praiseworthy——think about such things.

Read All About It….Twelve

PROVERB 3:7-10

3:7....Do not be wise in your own eyes; fear the LORD and shun evil.

3:8....This will bring health to your body and nourishment to your bones.

3:9....Honor the LORD with your wealth, with the firstfruits of your crops.

3:10....then your barns will be filled to overflowing, and your vats will brim over with new wine.

One Of A Kind

As the angels arose one early morn........Something special caught their eye
For the bowl of life was busily churning...............Atop of the Holy fire
And as they looked into the bowl.........They saw the potter's hand
Molding and shaping this woman of God.......To love as only she can.

It wasn't until they had a peep..........Beyond the wall of glory,
That their eyes expanded as they caught a glimpse...... Of her shining armor so holy.
Then God stepped back and in an instant....He knew this was one of His finest
For her worth is more...... Precious than gold....And His love for her was binding.

And as He gave a victorious sigh.......Amazed at the fire in her soul,
He gave a smile and threw the blueprints away.... And graciously tossed the mold.
Now she sits among us here.............Ready to lend a hand,
Always there whenever she's needed.........While living His holy plan.

MY SISTER IN CHRIST
AND FRIEND FOR LIFE....GWEN FULLER!!!!

Dedication

I would like to dedicate this book to the Glory of God. He has enabled me to continue to write his words. I give him praise and thanks for healing my body of cancer. Through Him, I am blessed and healed today. He let me know, that one of the stripes, that lay upon his back, carried my cancer to the cross. And He told me, in his word, that He would never leave or forsake me, and he never has.

Next, to my children, who put their lives on hold, making sure no appointment was missed, every prescription filled, no obligation left undone and most of all lots of T. L. C. was given. Thank you with all my heart, once again, you make me very proud to be your mom. And..... I thank you Father for the new arrival to our family, due in December. Hey everybody....It's a boy....Yeah!!!!

Now last, but far from least....The Cancer Center, and all its' staff, at Wesley Long Memorial Hospital, whose care and compassion was far and beyond exceptional. I give thanks to each and everyone, for their close attention to my needs, during and even after my treatments. Once again, I say "Thank You" with much love.

CPSIA information can be obtained
at www.ICGtesting.com
Printed in the USA
BVHW052123140223
658501BV00012B/228